TO: _____

DATE: _____

Welcome to the world!

100

good wishes

FOR BABY

MINA PARKER

This book is lovingly dedicated
to Bailey, Roman, and Luca

First published in 2007 by Conari Press,
an imprint of Red Wheel/Weiser, LLC
With offices at:
665 Third Street, Suite 400
San Francisco, CA 94107
www.redwheelweiser.com

ISBN: 978-1-57324-312-4

Library of Congress Cataloging-in-Publication Data
available upon request

Cover and book design by Kristine Brogno
Typeset in Memima, Avant Garde, and Avenir
Cover illustration © Kristine Brogno

Printed in Hong Kong
GWP
10 9 8 7 6 5 4 3 2

introduction

The arrival of a new baby is a reason to celebrate, rejoice, remember, and make plans for the future. It's an occasion to wonder about who the baby will be and to share wishes for every good thing in the coming months and years.

In parts of northern China, I am told, there is a tradition of making a one hundred good wishes quilt for the new baby. It is crafted from squares of fabric given by family and friends with their hopes and dreams for the child. Around the world today, these quilts are often made with companion scrapbooks, where the wishes are collected together with bits of the fabric for the family to enjoy. I like this tradition so much I decided to make a book full of the wishes that I have heard and collected over the years, a book to welcome a new baby into your life, and to wrap this child in the warmth of your love.

When I was born, my friends and family made a quilt. I loved it to bits (quite literally), and I still cherish the pieces that are left. It was a collection of drawings and words on scraps of fabric from my godmother's trunk, plus all the love it took to make it. In my mind, this book is a quilt—wise words from people around the world and throughout time, paired with a hundred good wishes for your new baby.

"Listen to many, speak to a few."

—WILLIAM SHAKESPEARE

wisdom

fun

Rollercoasters. Ice cream. Silly songs while
Dad does the dishes. May you have fun in all
the ways you expect and a bunch of ways you
never imagined.

silliness

Sometimes the fastest way to get there is
hopping on one foot with your tongue sticking out.

abundance

"Love is a fruit in season at all times."

—MOTHER TERESA

Sleeping through the night—a fine achievement for baby and mom.

achievement

inspiration

"A mother's love is like the tree of life, strong in spirit, peaceful, wise, and beautiful"

—AFRICAN PROVERB

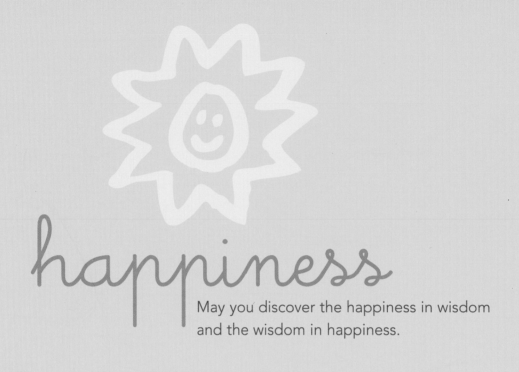

happiness

May you discover the happiness in wisdom
and the wisdom in happiness.

hope

"Learn from yesterday, live for today, hope for tomorrow." —ALBERT EINSTEIN

"I meet my work with strong limbs, open hands, proud heart." —SHEA DARIAN

energy

calm

"May serenity circle on silent wings and catch the whisper of the wind."

—CHEEWA JAMES, MODOC TRIBE

freedom

Barefoot in spring grass.
Running without your diaper.
Living the good life.

music

"The only thing better than singing is more singing." —ELLA FITZGERALD

willingness

. . . to take one more bite. To lie down for a much-needed nap.
To listen to mothers who sing off key.

spunk

"Find out who you are and do it on purpose."

—DOLLY PARTON

Whoever you are, whatever you do, may you be you.

uniqueness

"Sometimes questions are more important than answers." —NANCY WILLARD

curiosity

"Nothing in life is to be feared.
It is only to be understood." —MARIE CURIE

insight

strength

So big! So strong! Stretch up to the sky!

independence

"A mother is not a person to lean on but a person to make leaning unnecessary." —DOROTHY CANFIELD FISHER

chance

"If you don't know where you are going, any road will get you there." —LEWIS CARROLL

love

Giving and receiving, coming and going, now and later,
may love surround you always and all ways.

good fortune

"There was a star danced, and under that I was born." —WILLIAM SHAKESPEARE

"To watch us dance is to hear our hearts speak."

—INDIAN PROVERB

lightheartedness

Skipping, hopping, stopping to take the world with a grain of salt.

"Perhaps they are not stars, but rather openings in heaven where the love of our lost ones pours through and shines down upon us to let us know they are happy." —ESKIMO PROVERB

legacy

trust

Don't worry, Mama will be back and
she'll scoop you up in the biggest hug.

individuality

"The child must know that he is a miracle, that since the beginning of the world there hasn't been, and until the end of the world there will not be, another child like him." —PABLO CASALS

Follow the spring in your step.

spirit

"What is called genius is the abundance of life and health." —HENRY DAVID THOREAU

May you always have all of what you need and plenty of what you want.

prosperity

caring

"Children are the purpose of life. We were
once children and someone took care of us.
Now it is our turn to care." —CREE ELDER

charity

"Giving is the highest expression of our power." —VIVIAN GREENE

drive

"Don't be satisfied with stories, how things have gone with others. Unfold your own myth." —RUMI

Gentle, gentle. Share a story, kiss a hurt.

kindness

responsibility

"If you want your children to keep their feet on the ground,
put some responsibility on their shoulders."

—ABIGAIL VAN BUREN

politeness

"Manners are a sensitive awareness of the feelings of others.
If you have that awareness, you have good manners, no matter what fork you use."

—EMILY POST

determination

"There are no shortcuts to any place worth going." —BEVERLY SILLS

hard work

Rolling over. Sitting up. Creeping and crawling, standing and falling.
Walking, too. Lots to do!

"The road to success is always under construction."

—LILY TOMLIN

resourcefulness

resilience

"We may encounter many defeats but we
must not be defeated." —MAYA ANGELOU

Putting the puzzle together piece by piece. Good job!

concentration

goals

"Always remember, you have within you the strength,
the patience, and the passion to reach for the stars
to change the world." —HARRIET TUBMAN

talent

Twirling. Trilling. Strumming. Humming. Ta da!

lifelong learning

"Intellectual growth should commence
at birth and cease only at death."

—ALBERT EINSTEIN

"The most interesting information comes
from children, for they tell all they know and then stop."
— MARK TWAIN

beauty

"The most effective kind of education is that a child
should play amongst lovely things." —PLATO

nature

May you climb mountains and swim in the ocean.
May you breathe the freshest air and drink the clearest water.

growth

"May your life be like a wildflower,
growing freely in the beauty and joy of each day."

—NATIVE AMERICAN PROVERB

connection

"All people are my brothers and sisters,
and all things are my companion." —CHANG TSAI

On a warm day: butterfly kisses from your best friend.

On a cold day: a perfect snowflake coming to rest on the tip of your nose.

gentleness

family

"May you always know
your family as your safe
and good home."

—MARY ANNE RADMACHER

bliss

Fast asleep in Grandma's arms.

dreams

"Learning to understand our dreams is a matter
of learning to understand our heart's language." —ANN FARADAY

"The best and most beautiful things in the world cannot be seen or even touched. They must be felt with the heart." —HELEN KELLER

sensitivity

The softest blankie, the coziest snuggle, the biggest hug.

warmth

joy

"May there always be sunshine! May there always be blue skies!
May there always be Momma! May there always be me!"

—LEV OSHANIN, "MAY THERE ALWAYS BE SUNSHINE"

Peek-a-boo! Go fish! Tag, you're it! Yay!!!

games

wit

"When you are dealing with a child,
keep all your wits about you and sit on the floor."

—AUSTIN O'MALLEY

humor

"Blessed are we who can laugh at ourselves
for we shall never cease to be amused." —ANONYMOUS

magic

"Above all, watch with glittering eyes the whole world
around you, because the greatest secrets are always hidden
in the most unlikely places. Those who don't believe in
magic will never find it." —ROALD DAHL

luck

"Remember that not getting what you want
is sometimes a wonderful stroke of luck." —DALAI LAMA

ingenuity

May your mama be one step ahead of your schemes. (But only one.)

"Show me the path where I should go, point out the right road for me to walk. Lead me: teach me." —PSALM 25:4-5

education

skill

"My mother's love for me was so great that I have worked hard to justify it."
—MARC CHAGALL

awareness

Of the whole wide and wonderful world at your fingertips.

elegance

"May we walk with grace and may the light of the universe shine upon our path." —ANONYMOUS

wonder

"The sweetest flowers in all the world—a baby's hands." —SWINBURNE tranquility

A sleeping baby is a thing of beauty.

stillness

"Do as much as you can and take it easy." —TARA TULKU

shelter

A blanket fort on a rainy afternoon. A bit of shade under a beach umbrella. The warm embrace of your grandmother's hug. May you find a piece of home wherever you are.

bounty

"May you live as long as you want and
never want as long as you live."

—IRISH BLESSING

gratitude

"Gratitude preserves old friendships and procures new."

—ANONYMOUS

friendship

"What is a friend? A single soul dwelling in two bodies." —ARISTOTLE

forgiveness

For brushing the tangles out of your hair,
for putting you down when you're not at all sleepy,
for all those things that mothers will do.

"Peace is not something you wish for; it's something you make, something you do, something you are, and something you give away!" —ROBERT FULGHUM

courage

"How can you hesitate? Risk! Risk anything! . . .
Act for yourself. Face the truth."

—KATHERINE MANSFIELD

honesty

May you seek the truth and share it.

"Be lamps unto yourselves;
be your own confidence.
Hold to the truth within yourselves."

—BUDDHA

community

"As the sun illuminates the moon and stars,
so let us illumine one another." —ANONYMOUS

daring

"Whatever you can do, or dream you can, begin it. Boldness has genius, power, and magic in it." —GOETHE

Babies challenge us, and we return the favor.

challenge

zip

Strollers, tricycles, rollerskates.
(Pretty soon you'll be asking for the car keys.)

charm

"I have witnessed the softening of the hardest of hearts by a simple smile."
—GOLDIE HAWN

laughter

Smile. Giggle. Snort. Chortle. Breathe. Guffaw. Fall down in fits of laughter. Repeat.

"Whatever we are waiting for—peace of mind, contentment, grace, the inner awareness of simple abundance—it will surely come to us, but only when we are ready to receive it with an open and grateful heart."

—SARAH BAN BREATHNACH

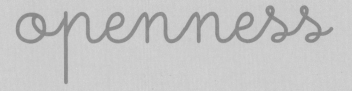

gusto

Life is good. Slurp it up.

blessings

May your life be blessed.
May you pass your blessings along.

wealth

"Ordinary riches can be stolen, real riches cannot.
In your soul are infinitely precious things that cannot be taken from you."

—OSCAR WILDE

Sharing soggy bites of crackers and gooey kisses.

giving

generosity

"Thousands of candles can be lit from a single candle, and
the life of the candle will not be shortened.
Happiness never decreases by being shared." —BUDDHA

plenty

Oodles of hugs, tons of kisses, and love to share.

travel

To every continent, or just down the road,
may all your journeys be wonderful.

history

"Family faces are magic mirrors. Looking at people who belong to us, we see the past, present, and future." —GAIL LUMET BUCKLEY

glee

Mama blowing on your tummy, Daddy dangling you upside down.

health

"We can know the future only in the laughter of healthy children."

—ANNE WILSON SCHAEF

Juice! Yogurt! Apple bits! Here they come . . .

anticipation

heartiness

"In a child's lunchbox, a mother's thoughts."

—JAPANESE PROVERB

Eating your finger food one piece at a time.
(Until you stuff in a fistful all at once.)

refinement

balance

"Blessings and Balance, Balance and Blessings, for from Balance comes all Blessings."

—GRANDMOTHER KEEWAYDINOQUAY, OJIBWAY MEDICINE WOMAN

contentment

A nice hearty burp. Nuzzling into Mama's neck. Baby happiness.

truth

May you always tell the truth and may you always
be able to hear it, even when it's hard.